T0196293

Fragile Heart
A Pool of Dirt

KAREE STARDENS

authorHOUSE®

AuthorHouse™
1663 Liberty Drive
Bloomington, IN 47403
www.authorhouse.com
Phone: 1-800-839-8640

Published by AuthorHouse 12/13/2012

ISBN: 978-1-4772-9778-0 (sc)
ISBN: 978-1-4772-9779-7 (e)

Pictures as taken by Courtney Madria Steven

I dedicate this book to my Lord, Jesus Christ who gave me this fragile heart. I hope one day my life will be a testimony of healing and grace and true love.

Contents

Bitter Tears

I cried and every tear
Stung both eyes sore

I cried and my body thanked
Itself for letting go

I cried for yesterday and today

Woe be to the one
That is thrown away

Woe be to the one
That stands alone when she cries

Woe be to the beauty
and laughter is diminished

Woe be to the one who dies unnoticed

Woe be to the young
That withers away in youth

Woe be to the one
Whose tears fall silently

Even though they scream out loud

Woe be to the smallest child
carrying out the curse

Woe be to the one
That doesn't want strength

Woe be to the one
That has never been loved

Thus far it seems,
Woe be to me

Stolen Pearl

Tiny white shine
Accenting my brown

Held rocking
Right in the palm

Such a big smile
Is what you gave

My favorite jewel,
My one accomplishment

Just like that you were given –
Just like that you were taken

I am at a loss
But do not count it forever

You made me unique
Am I supposed to mourn?

My little pearl was stolen
Perhaps a borrowed gift

I should feel lucky
To have held the little thing

Change of Pace

Running, racing, trying, achieving
Catching up was number one

Panting air, quickly thriving
I may not stand a chance

Breathing hard, stretching limits
Muscles sob but iron wills on

Crunching shoes scold within it
Because this race is a song

Sometimes time stays still
Even though blurs come undone

Spinning around at odd tilts
Deep breaths block the next thought

Deeply in and out until lungs overfill
A change of pace will keep it fun

It's okay to sleep or think a while
Just rest and dream while they run

Sooner or later they'll sleep, too
And hard work makes you strong

"A change of pace
Can do no wrong"

Said the turtle to the rabbit
I'll let you guess who really won

Crying in the Pumpkin Patch

Big dance with a love for all
I was invited to that ball

To watch the ladies
Dance with ease

Dressed like dolls
For this cause

The men came graciously
And added to the scenery

One by one they said goodbye
Each pair had starry eyes

Even *she* found a lover
And *I* sit a little lower

Time is ticking quickly;
The sand is quite slippery

Will he finally come tonight?
Will anyone notice my plight?

Am I destined to cry alone?
In the garden time takes the toll

I kneel beside the smashed pumpkin
The nothing that was a something

Even it was glorious tonight
In its final moments before it died

My tears fall, so unheard
While mother laughs at my curse

No angels come to save
No prince or horse to claim
No knight in shining armour
No kiss before the harbor

It seems I'm meant this way

Torn dress, longing for the day

Crying in the dark
Even the mice pull apart

Hope for joys cannot begin –
And the other three seem to win

Is it true, the balls shows the final scene?
Why do I want to walk in?

Perhaps I ought to be happy
Washing dishes

But I dared to hope that life
Had more to offer tonight

Blissful Way Down

So many sunny days
Lined up in a row

Not too far to count
But enough to seem that way

It is not when the leaf
Hits the ground

That my chest can relax
And cave in

It is how the leaf falls
That fills the cup with peace

Older Sister

You don't know
that you are beautiful

So you try too hard
to be intimidating

Even though it kills your insides
and bleeds onto your pages

Your guts churn
with who you aren't

But sister, as dark as you choose
You are still beautiful to me

So go ahead and loathe me
A learned behavior from small

Because of your own fear
to break the mother wall

I still hold you in good esteem
But know that you don't frighten me

Quest for Love

Calling, searching, dreaming
Always running against traffic

Longing, wrestling, striving
Dreams of reunion

How I yearn to experience such love
If even in one breath

Watching, seeing, disbelieving
Only movies have good ties

Fading, changing, chilly
You no longer smile at me

Rusting, crumbling, dirty
To stay forever this way

Please tell me it's not done

Seeking, dismissing, running
No man is good enough

Until he bends two knees for you,
One knee before me,
Ever sincerely

Wishing, wanting, wondering
Is anyone else searching?

Waiting, daring, hoping...

Please tell me something more

Uncertain Child

awkward moment

bend the knee

bite the nail

and wiggle the toes

inside the shoe

big eyes stare

lashes curl

shy, not scared

standing still

sometimes knowingly

uncertain of

proceeding steps

like a child

wanting to suck thumb

gentle hands

open hearts

two-way streets

and blessings new

tied with songs

to meet the needs

reaching out

blind in dark

but inside sobs

skip a beat

not too far

tilt the ankle

bite pinkie nail

standing still

unsure of how

Almost invisible

Walking through the lonely alley
shadows and questions whisper:

"Will my heart be whole?"
Loneliness pierces my soul,

Through the flesh and to the heart
which burns the days away

My eyes fall at cheerful tones
"merry Christmas!" was well meant

I do not wish the same
damage on you

Family, love and peace combined
was ripped away from this child

Never truly loved, feeling it today
Season joys were not meant to be held

Rumored to be beautiful,
That, too, lost its magic years ago

I wish to go back for a while
to learn to stop the hating

I wish I was a child again
so my cries could be heard

Performing and giving
provides slight sparkles

As soon as the last song ends
those moments fade away

Tug-of-war emoticons
Far from floating snow

Sinking below black ice
"When will this be done?"

Will today's dawn meet my needs
only once I die?

In heaven there'll be no worry
So my heart sings for it daily

Jesus should be year round, folks,
not once upon a year

Christmas is no longer about Christ
It just adds to the heavy yolk

"When will my heart stop hurting?"
I'm quickly losing hope

Little Child

little child
across the way

please take this,
a loony a day

when it has converted
you know the worth

I hope it helps
to stand the door

living child
across the waves

perhaps the while
took its shine

as a simple wait
to see your gait

I sincerely tender
it without tears

little child
across the way

I hope to meet you
one sunny day

In My Heart

A simple smile
Big sad eyes
In my heart I was screaming

A lonely while
Big bad eyes
In my heart I was fearing

A little time
Big glad eyes
In my heart I was dreaming

One small smile
Big sad eyes
In my heart I am healing

Fairytales Don't exist

Fairytales with happy endings
Castles and horses...
and of course, the prince

Each girl with dark moments
To be noticed and loved
Sought and brought to the light

To dance forever under stars
In gowns of rich beauty
To forget the woes of yesterday

So why am I in the back room
Crying in the dark and
Peeking under the locked door?

Where is my prince
or even the white horse?
Why do I wear such filthy rags?

No matter how I try
the dirt clings stubbornly
The water is cold, not warm

But the ball draws nigh
and I am so unsteady
How could a treasure notice me?

Family and friends, love and joy
Those cards left my hands bare
The queen of hearts spayed them all

Do I fold or keep hoping for a draw?
I want to crawl into that hole with the bunny
because I've seen that fairytales don't exist

Beautiful

They say my face is beautiful,
Why don't they leave it alone?

They say my songs are beautiful,
They are distant echoes

I'm told my eyes are lovely –
Better welled with tears

My laughter is your pleasure
To steal through the years

They say my face is beautiful
But it has turned to stone

They say my voice is beautiful
They can't let it go

I'm told my smile is lovely
When it bursts into tears

It is said my hair is gorgeous
Until it quakes with fear

What good is beauty
Always tossed about?

What good is beautiful
if you don't have love?

That Hand

Peering out the window
Into serene blowing nights

Behold there in the sky
Your hand beheld the moon

A bright, glowing sphere
Moving around here and there

Open for all to see
And all to appreciate

It was that same hand
Which cradles the moon

Once quickly saved my life
The same hand that wounded me

Falling Chills

It was cool when I stepped outside
Icy winds pierced thru my sweater

I trudged on anyway,
Taking the long way home on purpose -
Perhaps this will strengthen me inside

You died right before my eyes,
Plummeting to the street

I watched you swirl down gracefully
Unaware that I saw

I vowed to walk across town that day
Perhaps on the way back I'll wear that fleece
In order to properly keep my promise

Cutest Little Ribbon

Cutest little ribbon
Tied to a tree

Glitzy ribbon
On plain sight

Cutest shiny ribbon
Sparkling at me

Nicest little ribbon
Smiling up at me

Not flashy or large
Just the right size!

Deep in thought

Is it better to be loved
and have it stripped away
than to not be held at all?

I choose to walk on the ice
just to be different
and to strengthen my core

You kept this child safe
even though I cried out
and lay the pills before me

A huge decision to make
but still with angel's wings
guiding me home at night

My heart knows to hold on
God, you go by many names
and you see and know everything,

But how can I approach you,
who asks to be my Father,
about things you don't think about?

Let the songs
        wash over you

like waves
        in the night.

Live for the
        electric wail
            of guitars
    that caress
            your heart.

Don't you dare
        forget
    who you are.

The Turtle

I was an invisible
Frail, little child
Kept in the dark

I was a tear-press
Used to fill vials
Saved for Judgment Day

I was weakened
Unable to get by
Or to stand up at all

Now I am slower
Always running hard
Just to stay awake

I am the turtle
In this race of life
The hares dare not break

Although now feels solo
And much harder underneath
I am not a garbage can

For I have been chosen
To "win" the race
By the efforts of my guts

Puffing along the path
My shell grows heavy
And sweat leaks into my eyes

Still, I plunder along
The rabbit speeds ahead
Laughing at my woes

He hops on so freely,
Leaving me in his dust
But one day soon

If I persist

Should time be on my side,
I will pass my sleeping opponent
And claim the right to win

New Wishes

Old wishes
Lose their glimmer

No longer
About yesterday

No more stove
Constantly on simmer

My hand relaxed
And you fell out

You were black
And I was blind

It has ever been
Too hard to hold

So I let you fall
The penny that shattered

You spilled your luck
And time ran behind

Face up to the sky
Eyes grace the clouds

Feathers fan
With nostalgic blue

Take me to where
New dreams come true

As simple blades of grass
Don't let me freeze now

It's time to be aware
I'll carve this sign for you

So that when you shout

I'll follow you home

Content

Little lilac
Sweet powdered charm

Little lily
Drifts on the frozen lake

Birds chirp with me
The sun beams are warm

Clean, crispy air
Makes it easier to breathe

Clouds part the sea
Make it easier to see

Tiny rose
Scared to be close

These fuzzy feelings
I am finally home

Wondering About Wisdom

You were so cold
that I froze when I looked at you

you turned your back
which still conveys the truth

Shut your books away
and take the stride of wisdom

who shouts on streets
You who shrieks in public -

what do you look like??

I can hear you loud
but can't recognize you in the crowd

Aren't you drawn to me,

You, the one I seek?

You

You never forget me
even when time bolts past

Your hand is at my back
through that guiding wind

You blew against the ice
hard enough for me to try

I thanked you twice
because I realized

That YOU are my parent –
looking after the lonely scone

So count the strings on the fret
but one day please just let it soar

Innards long to feel that sincerity
enter the arts adored

So like the sport it takes a while
to quick the speed and stop the falls

Clocks tick while efforts tighten
but impossibility does not stand tall

That mountain sat on my liveliness
looming ominous and forbidding

But somehow through ice was the word
that to go unprepared will be hurt

You have presented a choice gracefully
and though I whine, you know to knead

So prepare me to climb –
wind the path up and around

Perhaps one day you will show the sky
and the view from above looking down

Help me to do all that you dreamed
in the venue of my deepest sleeps

To Make it Right

If I want to show you
I fall beneath the shadows

If I cry out loudly
a whisper drowns it out

If I search on all fours
it seems they stay outside

My heart pulses through my chest
And my tears are so bitter
they sting my face

Falling out,
Not running down

When I fear and am alone
I can feel your guard

When I try to give back
it goes all wrong

You give me the necessities
to stumble through each wake

But I cannot wield the knife
with these pleas for you to take

Can't you see it's barren?
Can't you feel the throb?

Yet when I look around
over my pain and through

I cannot help but realize
that I am the lucky one

Please don't bid me to die alone
it's hardly life anymore

There's so much unknown
I didn't mean to hurt you

I've turned around so far
and pushed away so much

But I cannot shake the solitude
while the crowds flaunt their lunch

Tell me what must be done
and how to make it right

Free

I am free to be me
Thinking about family

They state blatant lacks
but still researching

I am free to be me
A safe little butterfly

I am still me
Those who care often disguise

I am free to be me
Chains are sparkles blowing high

I am free
to laugh up at the sky

I will be me
and I CAN choose my family

I am free to be me
and smile for Holy Trinity

Hopeless Tears

Hopeless tears
Bitter years

Deepest yearning
For wings to comply

Longing to fly
To be done today

Not that child, but
A child besides

Still dark fears
Not at all, I hear

Hopeless tears
Amid the cheers

The Tree

Great pine who has been hacked
Deprived of height you did not lack
The young saplings soon surpass
And you are humbled not at last

You who cannot bear your height
Who can't stand tall through the night,
You still house the beaks of flight
And stand so green beneath the sky

My heart reaches you, tree that's been hacked
For I know God has my dirty back
Even when I dream of spiders and hands
That aim for faces to be slapped back

Whether human force or nature throes
You were denied the pointed nose
But still you grow and release pinecones
Great green, you make a good home

On the Bench

Sitting on the bench in the blizzard
Allowing joints to grow stiffer

Knots of today and yesterday
So strewn are all thoughts of clay

Yearning to lean back on the earth
Because I know it won't hurt today

But I still slide on the ice
The weather bends and lies

There is nothing worse to fear
Than a snowflake in the ear

If I let you in through the door
You wouldn't contaminate the floor

Faith

Baby steps
On a cold day

All it takes
Is a word to say

Faulty steps
Along the way

Don't let it faze
Or get in the way

Trembling steps
Every day

Once more grace
And no more rain

Giant steps
On sunny days

The Befallen Mouse

Poor thing,
Little did he know
The troubles he would sow
When he picked it up
And began to fill his cup
Barking orders to and fro
Iron and spears
He began to throw
Screeching this way and that
Making them flee as if gone mad
He never looked himself
Although you couldn't tell
Through fire and cast on walls
It loomed enormous, it stood tall
He wasn't the only one, though
To be afraid of his own shadow

Poor little mouse
Little did he know
The troubles he would sow
When he stole the show

Grandparents

The best choice ever made
was to leap on that lonely day

At fifteen I learned to gamble
and you helped me to be happy

You guys never put me down
and that is why I came around

When I was wounded by them
you stayed the same until the end

A pillar beheld in one eye
The two of you soothed those cries

The only one who knew my songs
You were keen to get along

Time was short and a bit too sweet
I am lucky to have experienced

Crumbling pillar, please don't leave –
live forever like we agreed

I wish that u both could be
in the lives of all my seed

A rough hand dealt by your clan
not your choice, I understand

Now you have withered
before your time

You have shrunk
to half your size

I cannot cry and crawl to your lap
I only stare and don't how to act

Good people is what you were
with my loyalty, I stand sure

I apologize on their behalf for
you and I know – they must be mad

To treat the best the way they have
I grieve today and you I'll thank

But deep inside we'll be okay
for I hope to meet you just the same

You said that you were proud of me,
but I am proud to have known you

You have given me all the strength
to not be ashamed of my last name

And you have shown great kindness

And treated me just the same

To see you crumble away

Hurts more than I can say

But if you need, I'll smile every day

Oxymoron

The sky bell's clear

But it snows outside

Snow on the ground

But the grass is green

In the midst of winter I wear my sneakers

You say this casual exterior

Is a rebel inside

Or tough skin

But I say knowingly,

You are the squirrel

That smells like peanut butter

To a dog

You could not be more wrong

I know how to clean well

But I couldn't be a treasure

So I don't know how to shine

My shoes were white

Til I strode through mud

No matter how I scrub

The sun looks down hill

The Accident

Speeding around the bend

Even both their lights

Said this was not close

They lacked severity

Even when the body swerved

And all the apologies

I'm glad no foot was hurt

A giant hand tapped the hood

And we all froze in the wood

It was the Highly Mighty

He knew what to do

With unscathed hares all around

We all know our worth

For God to show his hand

Even the edge of his sword

It had to be enough

For Him to agree without question

Twas no accident –

That is the lesson

Still a Hand

When the air is stale and still
Look at the treasures in my palm

Even when I turn to the sill
And think my work is gone

My eyes open their own will
To reveal more above to exault

Just when you think a hand is empty
It is too full to close

Mixed with dirt that shimmers
The jewels are mine to give

So I do until you have your fill
Almost to a fault

I like to look and see
That I can offer one last hope

Absence

Don't think for a second
The hands will unwind

When I am gone or you have left
Though you held my face between your hands

You twisted until it bled
And then kissed it all better

Don't think for a moment
That I'll be here forever

Don't walk upon the carpet you formed
When it prays to be swept away

Because those hands will stop
And the glass shards will scatter

There will be silence
As you gaze upon the bare penny's face

Abstinence

Blue eyes fade to gray
Don't ask why I ran away
I can't stay a piece of clay
In your hands, scared today

Wary eye behind kind smiles
Glance my way, worth the while
When I bled down that whole aisle
And pulled the knife with my style

You crept forth to split the yolk
Bent backwards did my soul
Around and around, still falling north
Even when that stops, I get so cold

Desire did stare at me
From your eyes, twinkling
I want to feel this freely
But oblivion has blinded me
Tell me it was worth the blood spill
Say that the skulls are killed
Share the strengths of my skill
Don't leave me atop this hill

The sweat of eternity is torn
Upon my brow the earth is shorn
So blow the bugle; sound the horn
A simple little grain of corn

Get out of my head if you can't stay!
To be together would be the way
But I'll never know if you don't say
So I stand, a kid, pushed away

The heart is under lock and key
He stole the plunder from the tree
The branches fell when I ran free
Don't let that story repeat defeat

A different man so worth the while

I wish I knew to take the time
With you I hold every dime
But even you haven't seen me cry

Heart and soul click right away
We sing, we talk, we laugh all day
Push the throes of love away
We were burned just yesterday

If your hand is mixing now
Help me know what to give and how
Don't let this flower pull under plow
To be crushed forever, broken vows

Let this be a two-way street
Finding joys each time we meet
Let it be open, not discreet
Oh God, please, please!
Let this be a blessed thing!

The Gift of God

To be held forever
In one palm

Spinning around
Life forever

Such gentility
So unknown
Yet it's common

Don't waste the hurt
But take the tears

The gift is yourself
If our eyes can see that

It's not the end...
Not this way

Going Round

The third time we passed the Second Cup
On the same street
The streetcar tried to wipe my face
But I couldn't hear a thing

Maybe he's running from terrible things
He did for the last time
Maybe she's shaken from good things done
For the very first time

Buildings whirl just the same
All the way downtown
In a straight line even my thoughts
Spin round and round

But when the bus stops,
It's not so easy to let go...
Or is it!

Which Side Do We Choose?

If death begets life then
why can't I heal your scars?

When ice fell from the skies
I felt how much we meant to you

Severity cannot gently peel
the slush from cement

The holiness of your face
surpasses our thoughtful threads

Your body and your robe
were stolen for the show

The bloody wounds ooze
and we wrinkle our noses

What a right you have
to judge the hands that

pounded the nails in
When I wear the stain of blood,

how can I deny my part?
In my mind's eye I hear you there

bent in weakness, covered in blood,

Rooted in spot, panting hard
looking to the end, like I try to

Just because dirt and blood mingled
entwined with the sweat we forced from your brow

Doesn't mean that in my own eye
you couldn't have a fresh body

You peer inside and say
"it's not the same"

If your eye is on the sparrow,
Where do your scars remain?

To Make Me Smile

A kind word
Wired over the web

Just to make you laugh out loud

Blue eyes behind
long eyelashes

Connect with mine in time

A warm beam
strong light

Sent to warm my soul

Hearts above
kids draw in the sky

God says that I'm alright

Is this peace?
It's so sweet

I can't believe it's here!

Wishful Thinking

Wanting to hold the gem
Forced to stare in its eyes

Even just to glide beside
And giggle all day long

I'll sing the songs of old
Mingled with tunes brand new

God it seems so hard to bear
But even in the darkness

You reached out your hand
And gave a music note to cling to

Like a child in the dark
So stained my skin is black

I just long for purity
A pirate, dancing in the wind

I long for purity
And to sing again

In My Loop

Round, purple, shiny white light, bright rocks,
Riches of this world are not intimidating.
Wooden glare, many bracelets, bobby pin, band stones,
diamonds,
This world's jewellery is not flattering,
So i look past,
If even at the floor.
It is snowing,
but the sky is clear.
I am wearing sneakers although i slip on ice.
No trees to bear the dandruff;
Let it be said aloud -

The earth is green, not brown.

Beneath

Soulful eyes
Nice to talk to
Someone alive
Feeling dead inside

Shred my heart
To be easier
Than hiding
These swells inside

How could the good
Like dirt and extra fingers?
Does he even notice
My efforts to be clean?

Higher intelligence
Even hangs over
Woozy with booze
Churning inside

Lay it all bare
Put the ball over there
Pressure on the valve
Not really fair, is it?

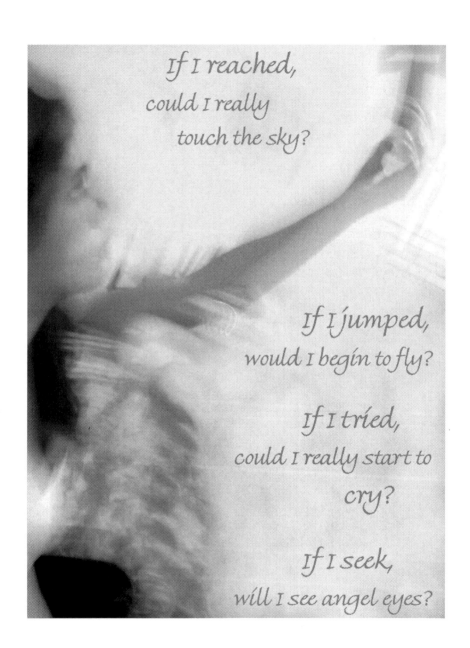

If I reached,
could I really
touch the sky?

If I jumped,
would I begin to fly?

If I tried,
could I really start to
cry?

If I seek,
will I see angel eyes?

Down and Out

Not too late at night
The sun pulled the blanket up

And began to close its eyes
But only for a while

Walking alone on the pathway
The trees creaked and groaned

But I wasn't nervous
Not even scared

The wind howled like the ocean
As it raked through the leaves

Lift them high,
Pull them out,
Twirl around
Until they bleed

The sky spoke to me last night
Through the shapes of the moon

You're only as troubled
As much trouble you let get by

I don't need their love
In order to love them

All the voices rush like water –
What lies they tell!!

I shouldn't even listen
But I wish for something softer

The stain on my face
Has sealed my fate

Dare I hope for change?

A Scab Like Me

Wishes don't come true
Not for scabs like me

How could anyone notice
The heart of a slimy frog?

A friend on the outskirts
is all I'll ever be

Yes, when I wished for bubbles
Indeed they turned into cages

Shiny bright surfaces there was
But dark and cold inside

I yelled and screamed
and thought I heard

A response that help was on the way

Well, from days to weeks to months and years,
I should have known better

Why wish to be rescued;
Why wish to be loved?

Wished don't come true -
Who would listen to a voice like mine??

Why dare to hope for treasure
when I can't harmonize??

Why cling to nothing
when I can't sink in??

What's the point of looking up
when my feet are on the ground?

No, wishes don't come true,
not for scabs like me.

Be Still My Heart

Be still my heart
no wait - just die!
Don't beat the blood
or curve the spine!

Don't love the bliss,
the rain or shine,
don't talk to the lungs
don't even rhyme.

Be still my heart,
leap from my chest
to be ripped out
would be easier felt

Too big to bear
I may just cry.
under weight
I'll stumble downhill

Be still, my heart
just don't try
Things you yearn for
can never be yours

Be still my heart
and know your place
Standing outside
Looking in on warmth

Cold blizzards turn blue
The wind pierces through
I shiver and want to cry
But I came so close, didn't I?

Inside looks warm
full of people and laughter
Fires aglow and sleeping cats
music and homemade food

But be still my heart -
just freeze for good
Make yourself turn away
for they have what you never found

What does she have that I don't?
Do not cry, my heart
Let go of hope
Love is for them inside

Not for a fool like me
Take a rest my heart
and know your place
Always outside, looking in.

In the Tunnel

I cry and sweat and bleed
I breathe so hard
My life caves in

My ribs pulsate
Faster than my heart
And muscles pulls away
From every bone

You said to be child-like,
So why, a child,
Can't you let me be?

When a soul has worked
It's depths and core
Inside out each day
Just to stay sane

What is left to grasp
When the world turns away
And laughs with her eyes?

Tell, me, what can I hold on to,
When I have offered my heart
For the very first time,
 And felt it denied??

How can I chase someone
That doesn't see my pain?
How can I pursue someone
Who wouldn't look my way?

Do you command my solitude?
Am I paying twice for sins
I skinned myself to atone?

Children are innocent
And carefree and loved
They are beautifully cherished
And energetic – almost magical

I am so weary from running
Running in the dark
Chasing things called hope

I am the empty one
Who was left alone
Crying outside in the lot
While she drove on home

You are all about family
But I have none to own
You are all about marriage -
Still nothing under that stone

If this child is not for love,
I need to know
Because to hope and yearn
Hurts so much worse

To feel unfelt is to be told
If not dual traffic,
I want no part

Guard the heart with no lock or key
I implore you, up there
To help me; hear my plea

Please don't leave me;
The only one in lost and found
It's not good for me
Lend here a fresh breath

Let there be one in this world
Who would actually hold my hand
I don't want to be the strong one
Because I can't to carry as I run

I have looked and have seen
That I want to know what love is
Please don't deny
The tears pressed upon this child

Crying in the dark cannot be all;
Pounding fists on walls
Screaming to no one's ears
This cannot be the greatest life

So let me live renewed life;
The kind I bled and sought
The kind that I reformed for
Just to show that I try

Don't you make me an outcast, too!
Don't restrain true love from me
If you are the expression of such
Surely one drop would fill this cup

I'm Ready

I'm ready to go
Ready to do things right
Ready to let go

I'm willing to fade
Only to ease the pain
Wanting to fade fast

Let my hour-glass shatter
Take time from my hands today
Let the sands crumble dry

I'm ready to fly
To keep the peace
With brand new wings

I'm ready to go
To a new dimension
Can I ever be ready?

Change in Me

Looking at the end of the day
The moon's eye stays open,
But instead of scorning, it smiles

The flower pushes above the ground
With lovely colors
I appreciate

I lift my voice every week
To songs I don't know
I can't believe this is my choice

A little fight whispers from beyond:
What is happening to me!
Why change this way!

A sneaky reformation
That crawled from under the bed
I am losing the self I clung to ever since then

Let Me Down

Hearts in the sky are so dumb;
Only highlighting why you are numb

I should see tear drops every day
And acid rain would eat my face

Fleshy chunks fall inside my bones
Laughter boils as grins disintegrate

You let me down, you fake hearts
Now my own heart yearns to fail

I chase death and beg to enter
But even its cape flees each day

So let me jump from the clouds
Let my feet touch the ground

Let me run away for real
If I come back, I'll stay this way

The Walk

Is it worth it to believe
When the skies deceive?

Is it worth it to suffer,
Watching your heart pulse
In someone else's hand?

Why do I still feel hurt
When he squeezes the blood out?

Why do I cringe in pain,
Even though it is the same?

Is it worth it to fly?
But I can't try anymore
My soul will just faint

Yet you prop me up
And string me along

Even still it tires you
It burns your scars and crumbles my heart

Yet you jaunt along,
Walking with me

My feet drag on the ground, useless;
I can't even stand

The way you hold me up
Begs the question:
Am I the cross that you bore?

Am I the mighty oak
Tied to your broken shoulders?

Is it worth it for you, then,
To hear this one call for home,

Or should I worship like the others?

You hold me up

And carry me along

Even though it kills you to do so;
Even though I can't see

What's in it for you?
What do you want from me?

How do I know to try
For one more minute -
For one more day?

How can I hold on
When my youth wastes away?

No more strength
Our will is up for sale
Too tired to look –
Is it worth another day?

Behind the Clouds

Behind those clouds are more clouds,
Really, I know because I live there

The sun filters through,
but it doesn't warm the soul

At least not today

Moodiness is a cue
that the rains won't shut up

Sometimes lightning gives a thrill
and thunder interrupts,

Sometimes the clouds nestle you

But more often than not
they drop you if you cry

And they are deadly
when they reach down from the sky

Behind the clouds is not dead
it's just cold and colder yet

Behind the clouds is not dead
but I'm far from home, cold and wet

The wind howls,
Whipping my soul back and forth

It is times like these
That I stay behind the clouds

The Flower that Droops

The flower that droops
is the one that cries

It can't even bear
to face the skies

The shame in its color
runs from the thighs

That day was so blue that
the tiny flower died

Seeking

Under the bed,

In the drawers,

Mountain tops

Through the storms

In my heart,

Said out loud

Deepest thought,

Inner soul

Every cell

Not good alone

Learning now

Hopeful still

Will it pay off?

Who looks to stay?

Lonely Dandy Lion

My heart is beaten
beyond recognition

Take it to replace
the scars on your back

Take it, please,
let it be retribution

Lonely little dandelion
- a smile upon the ground

Where is *my* smile,
have you seen it?

Yes, he is here
at the end of the day

I walk the path alone
...alone....alone.

when I run fast and far
I always come back

Just like the dandy lion
isn't really happy at all

So running away
is an illusion

I yearn to run
and not return

Lonely dandelions
sing sad songs

For everyone to hear
but they prefer butterflies

Don't shut your ears
Or feed them poison!

This little dandelion
will say goodbye

Fade to blue forever
before you knew the reason why

Is It Right???

Is it right for the pocket watch
to hold his memory?

Is it right for the golden chain
to laugh as it tarnishes?

Is it right to feel anger
at lack of remorse?

Is it right to rejoice
at cutting her grasp?

How do I walk on
receiving no apology?

Is it okay to not want to see
them who stole my safety?

Is it right to know the absence
as life leaves the battery?

Is it wrong to feel finished
and to not go back there?

Is it wrong to not want to see them?
I don't hate them...

Is it right to claim
the lifetime behind my fists?

Is it wrong to feel like this?

Is it wrong to want to
seal the door completely?

I distrust their words;
their mouths wound like swords

They live to break the one they hate
Their bloody flesh they discriminate

They know their wrongs,
make no mistake!!

Is it right for me
to want to move on?

Is it wrong for me
to not want a part?

Don't force the step
I'll run that much harder

It's not wrong to still feel hurt
and it isn't wrong to distrust

It is wrong to slam the door
Nice and loudly

I can't reject them
the way they did me...

So what can I do??
Where is the way out?

Even the skinny black hands
mock by stopping when I try

Like a good wife
I'll make my arms strong

And block their blows
Until they get tired

And I'll keep looking up,
Looking up

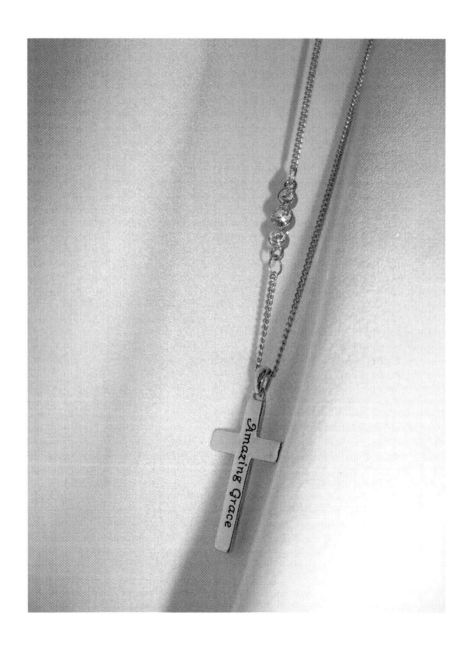

Your Picture

You think of me,
I know you do

You know I think of you –
You make sure I do

One step forward
Five steps back

But no steps back today
I'll stand still for a second

You glare at me
I know you do

But I forgot the effect
Until I saw you

The ever present storm cloud
Won't pass completely

Just seeing you
Reminded me

So leave my memory
Leave me alone

Don't get your glory
By my sorrow

Just a picture;
Gone in flames

Another Rainy Day

Rain pounds the window sill
As I sit inside

Tympanic revelation;
the earth cries all around

Grey clouds share my sorrow
as I watch their similarity

The sister who laughed was crazy
when I nearly split myself

The lady in that state
knew too many lies

Each raindrop weighs differently
but lands in the same place

Even the fish snaps,
wanting out like I do

But God gave a way
by letting there be no way

One day my eyes will peel open
and these sorrows will wane

The one who lies is one who accuses;
who knows what's true anymore?

Any drop could pierce my head
and slide right through my toes

For now they simply wash away
the beginnings I used to know

The earth dries itself
and I sob for what should have been

Another cloudy day
picked a good time

Another rainy day
to cry more tears tonight

For my older sister, May 31, 2012...At the Grave

Standing at the grave
I was cold with grief

Your feet were positioned
in cowardice

Poor little child
trained hard to hate

I doubt you ever knew
A day you weren't afraid

I long to take you
between forefinger and thumb

And place you as gently
as you can handle

Atop the safest seashell
Until you see that you're a pearl

You're not, like you think,
a decaying skull that stinks

So straighten up
and smile for real

Poor little child,
never really an adult

Clinging to his arm
you came respectfully

Poor wandering child,
I wish I could help

Fragile Heart

The heart flutters
and you feel something

for that person
But shattered like glass

the black bottle
held to the eye,

The slivers reap nothing
when they hit the ground

that's where they stay
The easiest thing to do

when your feet hit the ground
is to quickly run away

...but still...
The sunlight on the shards

glints so beautifully
who cares if it pricks my hand?

It may be possible
to fix this fragile heart

Your Choice

Shouldn't you be at home
stirring your cauldron?

You say "I'm not a witch"
but you certainly aren't a saint

You use people like puppets,
disregarding the throngs

That you hurt, destroy or burn -
but you're not sorry

I wish that you could see
how happy you would be

If you simply chose
to be a better person

The longer you hide in the tunnel
the darker it gets

Can you not see...
that you are the one chasing yourself?

So go on hating
or fearing me,

Chain me to the dirt floor
and cut my hair short

Deny my tearful eyes
but innocence glows bright

Darkness hides from light
and you will lie and fight

but you cannot have my heart
and I can't take the blame anymore

It's just not right –
That was never my place

Love

If this is the year of love
then let the rain fall steady
let it drown my sorrows
and stifle the drought
The one land is barren
but the scars on your back
have shattered my heart
so that I yearn for you
in the quiet slap.
What is it that I ask?
Will I ever know
this thing called love?

Out of Reach

You stand
I bend

Peering here
'Round a tree

Calling forth
Fill my ear

Familiarity leaves
In quickened pace

Eyes turn off
Spacey face

Sorrowed heart
Tender grace

Long eyelashes
Straighter teeth

Natural lips
To kiss the hand

No one offers
Chin is down

That's why I sit
At the well

Sorrow comes
Fills my face

Fleeting glimpse
Smile returns

Take my hand
Give an ear

I'll speak so soft
Then be of cheer

Smiles returns
But when it can't

You're not here
I'm out of reach

And I'm not coming back

Let Me Fall

A severe cut
Is enough
To look away from you

Dirty hands
On my knees
The sun scorches too

Nice big eyes
Full of tears
That I planted deep

Praying thoughts
Answered with
"That is why you're here"

Raspberries
And lemon drops
Leave me without fear

Let me sway
Tenderly
Graceful as the deer

Lonely petal
Far from home
Lead the others near

Somehow I know
Without a doubt
That you will meet me here

Conflict

I took a deep breath
and sank to the top of white

bubbles were the only jewelry
to wear upon my arm

thinking thoughts
do not feel better

fruit blossoms wither
at the sound of conflict

I work on my knees
but you only see dirt

bitter and sweet smells
both of them strong

not really mixing
thinking they'd relax

I wanted to laugh all day,
but you restrict my sound

if you swallow me whole
I will poison your insides

And while you live
You will want to die

The Black Day

'Twas the blackest day
turning away from songs

shadows suppressed my breath
their judgments tied me down

like a little blue flower,
how can I grow with a bloody sun?

Vendetta's in thrown knives
I hope you nail my heart

if I am so loved,
why am I invisible?

'Twas the blackest day
That centered the spotlight

And it was the blackest day
That showed me where to stand

Far removed…in the back
…fade to black

Waiting

The rain is falling again
tears my soul can't shed

I watch it mist outside
the world has turned to gray

am I dead while I'm alive?
Which man shall I wait for?

neither walks over
but both think of me

the rain is falling again
- testifying a broken heart

not just hurting for my own,
but for everything he owes

the rain is falling again
it slunk in so quietly

low clouds envelope the sun
stealing the rays of hope

the wind bears drops of ice
makes me glad I already froze

the rain is falling again
and I am inside looking out

funny how I wanted to dance
but no one would know

the rain falls outside,
revealing my personal role

so thrown off am I
that I don't even know

my duty is not a mission,
but just to sit and wait

it seems forever in the rain,
no choice but to wait

will the sunlight ever come?
Will I feel safe and warm?

Will the brightness hurt my eyes,
or fade away my scars?

How can I be ready?
I don't know what to look for

I guess I'll never know
unless I sit and wait

the rain is falling again
just like yesterday

I am waiting here,
Right where I was,

Looking out the window
just like yesterday

Silent Turmoil

Crawl into a hole and die afar!!
I'm as unclean as spit upon her seat

feeling stupid, feeling small -
it's not about color at all

how to find the words
to weep at the wall??

it wouldn't change a thing
I'd still sit outside tall

looking down my nose,
watching myself fall

I didn't realize the ball
bouncing back and forth

off the rackets
in the court

was my heart
so I'm done; I'm out.

Out of the game -
once and for all

my heart sobbed on the ground
threatening to quit all around

if I were to express in words
it would only upset the scores

and paint a dismal shade
to heighten the appall

I'm not half as strong
to stay invisible takes some gall

giant steps to permit the field,
but I wish I could erase it all

God leads you where your heart will break
but what if I can't even crawl?

I shook her hand and she was great
he likes her simplicity

we contrast, and it is hard
to flee the triangle without a part

how to be myself a treasure?
Will you run to the end of the hall?

The dark eyes are back, I've decided,
until someone makes them bright for all

The ice is back, too
Until there is reason to thaw

Metallic Vines

Metallic vines make their climb
Winding all around

Choking out the life
Smothering every sound

Metallic vines like barbed wire
Punctures deep inside

Thoughts tumbling all the time
No relief to be found

The leaves of poison grow with fire
To burn the hopeful crown

So they growl and they bite,
The filthy rotten hounds

Leaves with teeth alive
They kill and chain and bind

"Set me free!" is my cry
But the vines grow all around

Why can't I fly?
Why must I reach out?

Perhaps to stop the fight
Would end it all right

So I'll eat the berries from this vine
And choke to death tonight

Worthless

"Worthless child!"
Mother said since birth

"Worthless sister"
The siblings chipped in

"Worthless monster!"
Said those who can't relate

"Worthless bitch!"
From those who couldn't take

"I choose her"
He lifted the mallet

Smashing my heart

"Worthless to know"
Say the ones who don't

"She's not worth it"
From those who won't fight

"It's not worth it"
Said those who didn't help...

But why did they tell me?

"Not worth it"
From those who dismiss me

"What's wrong?"
Ask those looking the other way

"It really is worth it,
So stay here!"

Says unappealing emptiness
Another epic fail

"It is worth it"

Only when you get what you want

"It is worth it"
To rob my well being

"You are worth it"
When you make money off of me

Long term claims
Fail at the top

"You're not worthless!"
But history denies that...

The unloved prostitute;
No one cares if she's raped...

Is God really fighting for me??

Or is he the Father
Who looked away?

Nostalgic Hopelessness

Longing for happier times, while still happy-go-lucky self, inner smiles have withered, rendered painful because of loneliness that steals hope, the cherry on top of the worst pains - is this my destiny?? When I reach out, no one takes it seriously - so don't ask why I don't come to you. People are such a let down - so constantly, seeming to enjoy misery, not helping at all, not praying for true love, always confirming my solitary confinement...I wish it was over!

Why has God decreed so much pain for a child's soul? Where is the hope He has promised so many times? Will I die truly alone? When does this road end? When can I go home, far away from here; out of the earth?

Yet despite the shadows, I skip in the sunlight that I was forced to find as a means of coping, not crying, but hiding inside and withdrawing, coming alive only when the music plays...perhaps I, too, have been locked in a box, under the command of crank and wind...used only for the melody and shut away right after admiring eyes say distant "hellos," thinking that I have it all together. Why would God instill so much anguish on a fragile child? If my tears are important t o Him...are not my smiles of any value??

But some strange thing promotes a glimmer of hope - like, maybe all these daggers and cuts and dead-ends are preparation for something better, like maybe I wouldn't love what I get if I didn't suffer for it first - if even unknowingly...but how to keep hoping in something invisible?? Are those thoughts just delusions that I feed myself to survive?

I keep lifting my eyes to the skies and searching for help; how long to starve, watching others feast, before I can be full and rested?? How long before I'll *want* to live? How long until true laughter? Are my prayers unnoticed? Am I doing something severely wrong?

I know that God hears my pleas and weighs each tear to keep - but what else to say, if not to be redundant?? What else to do? The songs come out but they die quickly...perhaps I will bury myself in them and create a pearl for someone else to find. Yes, I know that God has seen and heard, therefore he knows even as he knew before...but...why such consistent aching? This pain is drives me to look down and drag my feet. How to grow underneath a black sun? Or am I really color-blind?

Unlucky

Sight everywhere is so confined
That I look without seeing

I depend on ears for safety
When crying out to God

The fragile heart shattered in the box
Stupid mail man...

The sender forgot to post the stamp
That day that grandpa died.

So I do not know where to return to...
But I can't let the twin come too close

Because it is unnatural
For us to be kind to each other

I was tempted to rip out my hair
When I became a fool

He did what I asked,
But I didn't think it would hurt

So I'll smash the remaining shards
And prefer to never feel again

Even though deep inside
I long for what they have

The child that never grew

Ran upon the daisies

Round and round
Little feet on the petals

Until the wasp almost ate thee
But you never feared the bumble bee

And one day she wished so hard
That she could grow and grow

So nothing could eat her
And no people would step on her

The child that grew
Slid down the stem

And stood under a leaf
But that wasn't enough...

So the child grew some more
And as she did, her soul weakened

Living life and smiling,
Looking without seeing

She grew to hate herself -
Such a cherished thing!!

But at long last that night
Curled inside a closing bud

The child sleepily opened her eyes
And saw that not all was lost

She is still and always will be
The sweet child that never grew

Burn it all until the end

Pictures, memories, hanging stars
Anger and angst again

Books and letters, music notes
Wonderfully wounding words

Burn it all until the end
Like leaves, like leaves

Anything left inside is dust
Don't deny destiny

Painting over my heart one day
Scars will smile, scars will smile

Let there be not one tear,
Burn it all until the end

Sorrows

Sorrows
Hang upside down

A widow
A red stripe all around

The boulder
Hit your heart now

At the bottom
You can only look up

My blood
Doesn't fill the cup

Touch
An angel's wing

And hope
To fly and sing

Before
You fade into nothing

Cry
Until each tear

Eats you
Slowly, deliciously

Thanks

Words I never said
Echo in my head at night
Words for all my life

Thank you for your hand
Pulling me out of death's grip
You set me down here

Thank you for ink wells
My sorrows befall the pen
So songs can hint a smile

Sad but not erased
In darkest of grotesque masks
More than just a stain

Memories might fib
Thankfully mine yell true words
They descend like snow

Thank you for a dream
Invisible in their eyes
Not always really here

Thank you for caring
You beat yourself and scarred me
But all for the best –
I know that now

Wish, wish

Wish wish upon stars
Heave a sigh gazing above
Can life mend this heart?

They call it life but
Why, why does it feel like death?
Let me sleep tonight

One year comes and goes
The leaves fall just like my youth
Losing color, too

Seeing happiness
In the eyes of all of you
While I cry alone

Sigh, sigh and sit down
No choice but to resign to
Never flying out

I hope when it's time
That I will soar mightily
Not hide behind doors

I hope for wide windows -
Will the sunlight hurt me eyes
Or will it feel warm?

Wish, wish just the same
Will there ever be a chance
To smile for real?

Will I ever hold
The bliss they never fight for?
Can I know if not?

Wish, wish, they move on
I'm the same old portrait left
Hanging on the wall

God tests you with time

Is anger fair if you fail?
I often do wish

To crash to the floor,
Splash broken glass everywhere
Cos tears do not heal

Like the ones who left
I am a memory, but
I am still breathing

Wish, wish it away
But it never really leaves
Those sorrows inside

Beautiful Rain

Beautiful rain
Wash my soul

Flood away
The memories

In and out
I feel so cold

How to grow
Beneath a lying sun?

You answer
With your sound

Each drop
Cries with me

And then I saw -
Things grow quietly

The Fantasy

To be held so warm
In gentle hands of deepest
Love rushing like waves

To pull me underneath
A tide of peace and safety
But I could not drown

I would fly so high
And see twinkles in his eyes
Twinkles that we share

It would be okay
To show him what no one sees
The inside of my heart

Inside my being
I would help him grow with strength
And he would guide me

This love would be real
And last through the fiercest flames
Of hell's deepest blast

One truly great man
That would not ashamed of me,
Nor I of him there

Standing beside me
A mutual decree
A mutual smile, too

I seek commitment
A timeless ring on my hand
A timeless true love

Fall Fall

Fall fall
before me
and beside me

fall fall
crunchy steps
crunch again

fall fall
wispy breeze
with a sigh

fall fall
bears lay down
for the blanket

fall fall
turning cold
turning seasons

fall fall
perhaps a change
of mine to make

Poisonous Tears

poisonous tears
cut as they fall

sitting at the grave
in the darkest night

we're so similar,
but now you smile

left alone this year
when you both fled

left alone again
without any worth

poisonous tears
tears of blood

full of fears
not enough

resembling the same
child that cried

glancing outside
in the black corner

I saw myself sore
I began to die

the last tear
slid down slowly

peeling my core
shredding my bones

that last tear
finally left my soul dry

Little Miracle

little miracle
that didn't know

still whole,
flesh and bones

still smiling,
wounded soul

those who didn't
did also know

little miracle,
letting go

saying "yes,"
rarely "no"

trying to reap,
trying to sow

the miracle is that
she doesn't know

they see her now,
their smiles aglow

fragile beauty,
a sparkling rose

through the snow
with a red nose

tiny lady
beneath your toes

tied with ribbons,
ribbons and bows

she's in their hearts
when hands have froze

mercy and grace
is what she tows

"little miracle!"
Shouts the crow

walking miracle
doesn't even know

Sometimes

In pitch black,
No longer tossing and turning,
No longer afraid

I stopped talking back
and stopped asking why
Because all of a sudden

I realized...I realized...

History will not repeat itself
and God holds me close
Because I am not dark!!

I am not dark!!

Sometimes and maybe, kind of
is all I get for answers,
But that's not enough

Still waiting but not turning blue,
I will breathe while I wait
to be alive if you come

I won't hold my breath...hold my breath...

But I'll still hope
and try to believe
as I pray

But I won't hold my breath, hold my...br...

Goodbye

Goodbye...
Sometimes is the saddest word to say
And it's sad to walk away
With just the memories

But I stride
With petals falling from my hands
And leaves crunching in the light
Promising my freedom

Let it slide
Was the hardest thing to do, yes
But history changed itself
When I made those choices

Broken blood
Oozed from the cracked skin
And my innocent body...
Until you were satisfied

You look fine
As you smile from day to day
But does he even know
The things you hide?

Are you happy?
I hope you finally rest
and have some harmless fun
Learn to be kind

Say goodbye...
Let me out of your mind
unclasp your hand from around me
and let yourself live

Say goodbye
For I shook the dust
From both my feet
As I walked away

Without looking back
So don't force my cheek
Don't stand and crow
Or it's goodbye forever

What I See

What I see is not meant for me
But she has he and he has she

But who have I
And who has me?

The lonely little bird
Flits from tree to tree

And sings a sad song
For those in need

Everyone claps at the end
And leaves so happily

After I shake hands gracefully
The road I walk is lonely

Don't let me die of a broken heart
Because even now it's threatening

At night I cannot sleep
And during the day I only weep

You think I'm strong but I feel weak
I'm not aggressive nor am I mean
Where do I belong?
Where do I fit in??

How to have faith
When I simply don't believe?

The path I walk is lonely,
Seeping through the years

But the grass is still green
And the sky is foggy

I walk an isolated path,
Not knowing where it leads

Perhaps somewhere on the way

We will meet by destiny

Here on the Isle of Innisfree
A sad song comforts me

Until I'll walk no more
But curl up to sleep

Now and then I wonder
If the grass is really green

The things I see
I learn from

Insomnia

Teasing, pulling, laughing
Stretching my eyes wide

I want to shut them both,
Losing consciousness for a while

Yawning, praying, hoping,
The slumber takes its time

My body yields right of way
But the soul stays awake

Tossing, turning, thinking,
Thought plague my mind

Taunting, laughing, whispers
Questions force a sigh

History and dreams collide
And I am forced to cry

Breathing, singing, praying
I finally close my eyes

One, two, three...
The sheep jump to high

Health, sanity, favor
Won't grant until twilight

Working, learning, straining,
Hopeful cause for sleep

I might relax tonight;
To sleep deep in peace

Safety, blankets, pillows
I'll count blessings tonight

Watch God protect me -
His favorite little child!
Listening, straining, silence

Sometimes I hear a lullaby

With his gentle hand over me
I'll finally rest all night

Jealousy

Jealousy eats my skin,
Rotting all my bones

Wearing my heart down,
Squeezing the blood out

Killing the good,
Destroying my soul

I look to the left
And see you be blessed

A hand-out again;
You get what I want

I look to the right
And see you happy at night

I look up and see myself
An ugly lump

Trying to shake free
Too afraid to leap

I look down
Because I can't look up anymore

Tears each night
Only heavy sighs

Every moment
A fight to stay alive

I just want to float
In peaceful harmony

To Let Go

To let go
Would be grand

Much more grand
Than the best piano

To let go
Would be freedom

To shake that thing
Right off my arm

To let go
Would be to open up

To trust someone
But I don't know how

To say goodbye,
I want to now

To let go
And be free

Won't someone help me
To let go?

The silence

Daunting and thick
Shutting you up

A pile of dirt
Thrown on top

A cry in the dark
A plea for a part

Tearstains
And folded hands

Driven to stay alive
Running out of air

Dying inside
And punished the same

Too much to hold
In clumsy hands

Too many stairs
For two left feet

Too much weight
For tiny shoulders

Too much straining
For soundless ears

Too many beatings
For a fragile heart

A cry, a shout
A prayer to God

No answer then,
No answer now

Losing faith
Losing life
All those words

Are not lies

They cannot be
When it's all I see

So in the silence
I try to breathe

I feel myself fade
And quiet down

Even inside
I grow quiet

Inferiority Complex

You rub it in
And I take the bait

Because I cannot see
What goods I have

You provoke
And pressure me

And shake your head
When I crack

So I pull away
And you lash out

Intentionally hurting
Because you're misled

You'll rub it in
Until I'm dead

You say those things
And don't take them back

You watch and see
And take when it's fine

But no support
When times are rough

You are right now
My inferiority complex

Because you build your shadow
To tower over me

In its entirety,
That's not enough

But you take and scorn
Each time I cry

You offer help
But when I ask

You make a show
And then say "no"

So tell me
What the point is

Of carrying on
And feeling like this

When you "can't help"
Or don't want to?

Go back home
Leave me be

For before you came,
I was flying free

Family

"We are family"
You say

But we aren't –
Not today

"Why are you like that"
You ask?

Because it's the truth –
Just look at my wounds

I suffered because of you
And I still suffer

Families love
Not threaten lives

Families talk
Not tear apart

A family ring
Should include everyone

So no, we don't pick up
Right where we left off

I seek freedom
From the connection

That keeps salting my back
The lashes you put there

With a smile on your face
While you spoke disgrace

You ripped my shirt
And pulled my hair

You stained my arms,
But not my face

You made me stare
Into your eyes

You made me know
Supreme hatred

What should have been love
Was only ever pain

And now I know
Exactly what you weren't

And family, family
Is what you are not

Redemption?

Words of a father
Who looked away;

Who never fought it;
Who never reached out

I had to ask before,
It must have echoed

Such a change –
You and I

You are likeable
Similar in nature

A kind man
Who made mistakes

You said "I love you"
And I want to know why

Father who looked away
And did not speak

You are hurting
And I wish it wasn't so

But that's no reason
To give another blow

I couldn't say it back
Because I don't call you "dad"

If you want to take it back
Step up and be a man

It is your turn to apologize
And to reach out this time

Look me in the eyes
And call me your daughter

Then, maybe we shall see
Where the roads will cross and meet

Home

Home for you is a house
With a dog and your spouse

Home for me
Is consistency

A walk at night in the park
Through the blizzard I stayed warm

A smile lit my path
Because I was home at last

Where the songs I sang
Matched the musical twang

And the lights above
Felt like enough

Even when they shine on everyone
It feels like it is your spotlight

Team work and celebrations
The goal is entertainment

And the stage…yes, the stage!
Offers a comforting space

Never in a million years
Did I picture myself here

Singing and dancing, nonetheless!
But, still, when I reminisce

This place steadily brings
The best of all memories

For once in my life
I can actually rise

And give what I have to offer
To the audience and to others

Not really my home to live in
But a place to laugh and fit in

A place where it comes together
And my feet are light as a feather

Where I beam
And feel complete

Every time I always glow
Because the joy overflows,

And the shows always show
That music really is my home

Convalescence

Life tugs and throws
Until I fight for my soul

God placed me in a cave
And covered it with his hand

He fights for me now
Because I was shot down

I feel the effects of the war
And cry out from the core

But such relief sealed
With time to heal

Jealousy infects
And rage interjects

But focus on the feeling;
Look at them like they are dumb

And when they leave…
You're not quite so numb

Freedom is my quest
But for now I'll rest

Freedom is my quest
And I will try my best!

Haunting

Haunting chimes
A minor third

Clear notes,
Comforting

Sadness inside
And on the street

Through the snow
It follows me

The wind howls
And flakes swirl down

The lights put up
Should be warm

But I have never felt
Anything colder

Christmas trees
And unity

My house is old
And no one stays

Like the stop sign –
Everyone leaves

But I still walk
On angel's wings

Past and present
Mingle now

To haunt my soul
And shred my heart

I sink lower
Than black ice

And the words
Circle 'round

Telling me things
I already know

I reach out in vain
Footprints come and go

Just like red lights
They speed away

The haunting here
Is my loneliness

The last day

Trumpets blast
Horns blow

Open seals
Poured out wrath

Burnt tears,
Swordfights

New amour
Flashing swords

Spilled blood
To satisfy

Tall shadows
Cracked earth

Sharp cries
Agony

Eaten scripts
Ink feathers

Disasters
All around

Justice promised
Restoration

The last day
Comes at night

No one knows...
Not even him

When it sneaks
Numbered days

Dices rolled
All face up

Cards lay bare
Goodbyes in store

Tears of blood
Washed away

Once and for all
Only for good

Redemption

I asked
And you said
But I shouldn't have
Had to ask at all

I sobbed
You looked down
Or there...anywhere
But over here

Silence
Stabbed worse
Than her evil speeches
But soft you speak

Invitation
With open doors
Just in case
It happens

Still staring
At many scars
I hesitate
And don't come in

Promises
Seem too good
And when that shows
It rings true
Redeemed
Loss of words
Rekindled bonds
So you say

They say
Actions speak
Louder than words
You have neither

Twisted years

Broken hoods
You still yielded
To evil ways

Dirty hands
Maybe not yours
But indifference
Still shouts

Father
You said it
When I didn't seek...
But why now??

Opened eyes
Baby kitten
Safe to trust?
Not yet...not yet

VICTORY – a cute little thing written by Cecile Corbiere in 1992.

He said to me:
"I want to quit farming...
get out of debt -
and get rid of you."
Ouch, that hurt!
Oh my, Oh my, my, my...
five children.

So the kids and I moved to wreckville,
visited some depths of depression,
and met with hopelessness.
We dwelt in despair, and
saw a lot of desperation.

The "TRUTH" eventually wandered by,
and gave us his key to "FREEDOM."

Hope finally came into my life...
like a beautiful sunrise.
All the rain that poured from my heart,
grew up blessings like patience and tolerance,
perseverance, gentleness and compassion,
and blossomed the most precious flower of all:

<<the JOY of the LORD>>
With Jesus there is VICTORY!
Thank You, Jesus! I love You!